SLUGS and SNAILS

Written by Robyn Green
Photographs by Kathie Atkinson and Densey Clyne

Acknowledgment
The author and publisher would like to thank Densey Clyne of
Mantis Wildlife for her advice on the text.

This edition first published in the United States of America in 1996 by **MONDO Publishing**
Published in arrangement with MULTIMEDIA INTERNATIONAL (UK) LTD

Printed in Hong Kong
First Mondo printing, February 1996
04 05 06 07   9 8 7 6

ISBN 1-57255-026-0

Originally published in Australia in 1988 by Horwitz Publications Pty Ltd
Original development by Robert Andersen & Associates and Snowball Educational

CONTENTS

A common snail moving along a mossy bank

GASTROPODS

All slugs and snails are animals without backbones. They are called gastropods. They have soft bodies, and use special muscles underneath to move themselves along.

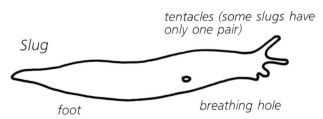

Slug

tentacles (some slugs have only one pair)

foot

breathing hole

Snail

the snail's stomach is inside its shell ("gastro" means stomach)

foot, with muscles for moving along ("pod" means foot)

A rain forest snail

A pond snail

A sea slug

Some gastropods live on land, and some live in fresh water, but most live in the sea.

SNAILS

All gastropods with shells are called snails.

This is a bubble-raft snail that lives in the sea. It hangs from a "raft" of bubbles on the surface of the water.

Land snails

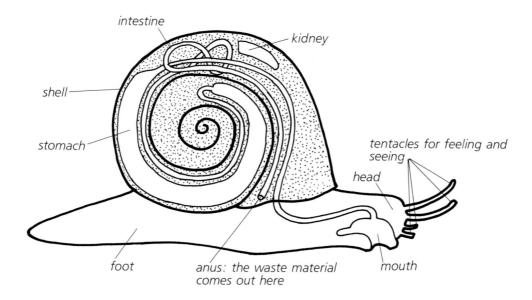

intestine

kidney

shell

stomach

tentacles for feeling and seeing

head

foot

anus: the waste material comes out here

mouth

The soft part of a land snail has a head at the front, a foot underneath, and the rest of the body is inside the shell.

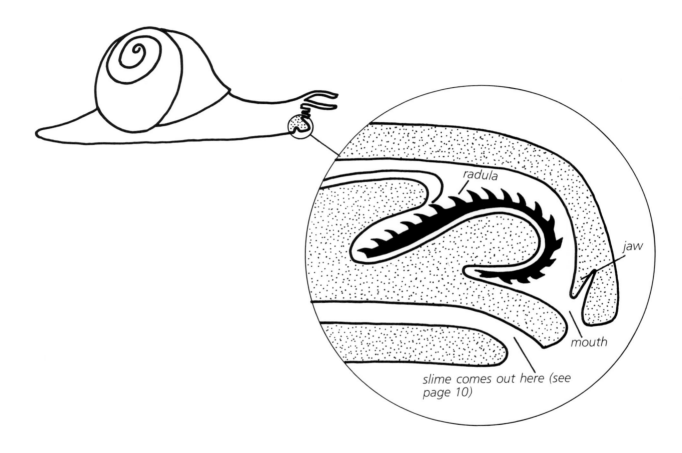

radula

jaw

mouth

slime comes out here (see page 10)

A snail's tongue is like a strap covered with thousands of tiny teeth. It is called a radula. Snails use the radula for scraping up food and tearing it to pieces.

Some land snails feed on fungi and some feed on other plants. A few feed on small creatures in their environment.

A plant-eating snail

Slugs feeding on puff-balls (fungi)

Land snails travel by making the foot muscles ripple. As they move, they put down slime from the front end. This slime helps the foot glide along.

A snail leaves a trail of slime.

*as the foot muscles ripple,
the snail moves along*

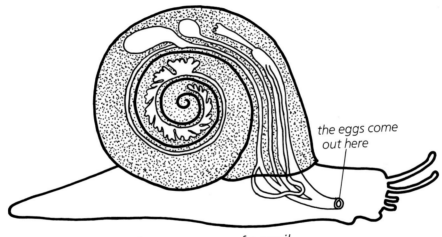

the eggs come
out here

The sex organs of a snail.

Most land snails have both male and female sex organs.
But it still takes two snails to mate and produce eggs.

After two land snails mate they lay eggs through an opening in the head. The eggs are usually laid in a safe, damp place.

Tiny snails hatch from the eggs. As the snails grow, their shells grow too.

Snails come out at night.

Land snails spend most days in damp, dark places. They come out to feed at night, or when it rains. Most land snails can pull their heads right inside their shells when they sense danger.

When the weather becomes too dry, most land
snails retreat into their shells and stay inside until the
weather gets damp again.

Water snails

There are many thousands of different kinds of water snails with shells of different shapes, sizes, and colors.

A pond snail moving on the glass of an aquarium

A cowrie moving in the sea

A bubble shell on the sea bed

An abalone

Snails that live in the sea are called marine snails. Many of the sea shells found on the beach are the empty shells of marine snails.

Snails that live in rivers, lakes, and ponds are called freshwater snails.

A triton shell

SLUGS

Slugs do not have shells. A slug's body is similar to the soft body of a snail.

This slug eats tiny fungi.

Land slugs

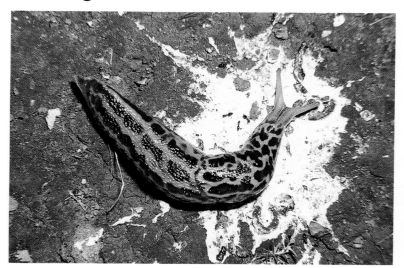

A slug feeding on bird droppings

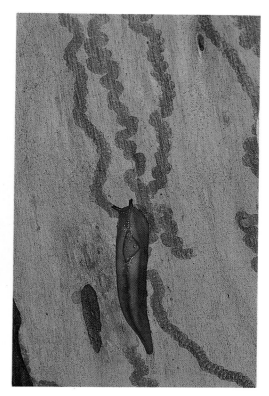

This slug eats plants.

Most land slugs eat plants. Some feed on toadstools and other kinds of fungi. Others eat dead plants and animal droppings.

19

Like most snails, slugs can be both male and female. Two slugs mate to produce eggs.

Mating leopard slugs hang from a tree on a strong thread of slime, and twist around each other.

Newly-laid leopard slug's eggs

Slugs also lay their eggs in a well-sheltered place. When the eggs are ready to hatch, tiny slugs crawl out fully formed.

You can see a tiny slug crawling out as the eggs hatch.

Sea slugs

Many different kinds of slugs live in the sea.
Their shapes and colors are wonderful.

A brilliantly colored sea slug from the Great Barrier Reef

A sea slug on a rock

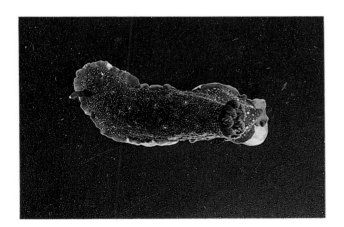

A sea slug moving in the water

INDEX

* means that the information on these pages is in the pictures only, and not in the text.